'Kidz Klubs

The Alpha of Children's Evangelism?

Philip Clark, CA

Minister at Trinity Anglican/Methodist Church,
Page Moss, Liverpool

Geoff Pearson

Vicar of St Bartholomew's, Roby, Liverpool

GROVE BOOKS LIMITED

RIDLEY HALL RD   CAMBRIDGE   CB3 9HU

Contents

Acknowledgements
Thanks to the Trinity Kidz Klub Core Team: Craig, Lizzie, Jane, Ed, Andrew and Steph and to Monika and Jean for their love, support, encouragement, patience and wisdom.

The Cover Illustration is by Neil Pinchbeck

Church Army and the Grove Evangelism Series
Church Army has over 350 evangelists working in five areas of focus, at the cutting edge of evangelism in the UK. It co-sponsors the publication of the Grove Evangelism Series as part of its aim of stimulating discussion about evangelism strategies, and sharing its experience of front-line evangelism.

Further details about Church Army are available from:
Church Army, Independents Road, Blackheath, London SE3 9LG.
Telephone: 0181 318 1226. Fax: 0181 318 5258.
Registered charity number: 226226

First Impression February 1999
ISSN 1367-0840
ISBN 1 85174 396 0

1
Introduction

In October 1998 six of us visited Bill Wilson's Metro Ministries in Brooklyn, New York. The week before we arrived they had registered 14,167 children and young people through their various ministries. In spring 1994 Frontline Community Church in Wavertree, Liverpool started a weekly club on a Saturday morning and adopted the Bill Wilson model of weekly home visits for every child. From 40 children a week, they now regularly have as many as 700. In Page Moss, Liverpool, part of Roby Parish, we amalgamated two after-schools clubs to start a 'Kidz Klub' with 50 children. Six months later at Trinity Anglican/Methodist Church, Page Moss, we regularly have over 100 children and visit 200 every week.

Is this the *Alpha* of children's evangelism? Like *Alpha* it has the potential to reach many who are unaware of the Christian story. It has a strong teaching element like *Alpha* and a strong relational element through the weekly visits, which every child receives. This high level of commitment is a key ingredient. Close personal relationships are built which help children to feel they are special individuals instead of just part of a large crowd. Like *Alpha* there is belonging prior to believing. Perhaps, though, the real connection may well be the potential for this outreach to children to be significant.

Unlike *Alpha* there is no small group gathering and Kidz Klub is not a nurture course. A key aspect is the long-term input into children's lives. A leader from Frontline visited a derelict block of flats in Toxteth. 'Broken glass, stench of urine, every flat was boarded up except one on the top floor. That's where Lee lived. I have faithfully visited him every week for over three years. Now he's in Secondary School, he visits the other kids with me every week. Faithfully in the cold and rain he's helping me bring hope to the kids on his estate. One day he'll be doing it on his own, reaching the next generation for Christ.'[1]

In New York Bill Wilson has been doing this for 18 years. The crime figures there include a drop in murders from 2000 to 800 a year. Credit for this is not without its takers—the Mayor, the extra police, and the 'zero tolerance' policy. Some of us have seen the impact of a ministry like Bill Wilson's and believe it is a part of the advance of the Kingdom of God.

Resolution 11.8 at the 1998 Lambeth Conference 'recognizes and celebrates the dynamic work of God among young people and their infinite value in the human family.' This booklet looks inside one such dynamic work. It asks how transferable it is from its American origins and whether it is a valid model of church. We have tried to outline some of the practical details of this ministry

---

1   Frontline Kidz Klub Newsletter.

but at the end of the day the most important ingredient is a burden for children. We have discovered that such a burden will find a way to tell the next generation that there is a heavenly Father who loves them. It seems, however, that the model presented here may just be the key that some of us have been looking for.

2

A Pioneer of Children's Evangelism

The Bill Wilson story has been written up in *Whose Child is This?* (published by Charisma Life).[2] Coming from a dysfunctional family, 'you wait here' were the last words Bill remembers his mother saying. She left the 14-year-old boy sitting near a bridge in a Florida suburb, walked away and never came back. For three days he waited until a Pentecostal deacon, Dave Rudenis, approached the abandoned youth and offered him food. Soon after, Bill went on a youth camp and that led him to follow Christ. This investment in Bill's life has borne tremendous fruit. The care and concern that was shown to Bill was never forgotten. It fires every aspect of Bill's ministry and means that he still drives one of the fifty strong fleet of buses and visits 120 children on that route.

Wilson's journey to the wastelands of inner city New York has not been easy. In Florida and Iowa he developed a Sunday School curriculum and adopted a strategy of 'publicize, visit, bring by bus.' He even started to develop a concept called 'Sidewalk Sunday School.' This involves using portable stages that fold down from the side of a customized truck. The leaders now take these vans out to areas like Harlem and the Bronx. They park the truck in a popular spot and put tarpaulins on the ground for the children to sit on. The programme then follows a similar pattern to that developed back at base.

When we visited Metro Ministries in Brooklyn, what did we find? First of all, a *truly exciting and dynamic work*. You cannot attract so many children without having a lot of fun. The church has a fleet of over fifty buses and each ride with a bus load of children was exhausting and lively.

Then in a converted brewery the children come for a live band, bigger than life cartoon characters, video, drama, games, prizes and a straightforward gospel message. One moment it is sheer bedlam, the next moment you can hear a whisper.

Whether it is in the Brooklyn Headquarters or sitting outside one of the

---

2   Available from Frontline Church, address in appendix.

vans that are taken out for Sidewalk Sunday School the ministry brings a real joy into these young lives. Drugs, violence, and messed-up relationships surround them and Metro Ministries is offering a spirit of celebration plus something that is safe, healthy and spiritually enriching.

Secondly, we found a *clear vision*. The team, including over fifty full-time staff, has a total belief in what they are doing. For them, reaching these children is truly a matter of life or death. They desperately want each child to know that God loves them personally. Each week they visit the children on their bus route or in the area of their Sidewalk Sunday School (see chapter on visiting.) They have been doing this consistently week in week out for years and years. They have a 'whatever it takes' attitude and nothing must deflect them from their children. A good job done at this age will save time later on repairing damaged men and women.

Thirdly, the *bravery and commitment of the staff* impressed us. On Saturdays, the first buses pull out at 5.30 am and then it is non-stop through three celebrations. It takes tremendous energy to keep up the pace of working with so many children and visiting them so faithfully. It also takes a lot of bravery. Bill Wilson has been attacked on various occasions including a brick in the face that almost cost him his sight. I asked one young, petite woman how she managed to keep going back to some of these blocks of flats with their various attendant dangers (she had just shown me a tree she had hidden behind during one shooting incident). Her reply: 'By the grace of God.' That same grace was taking another staff member to start a similar work in Vietnam. He fought in Vietnam as a nineteen-year-old and was now going back on a different mission. Bill Wilson has been in New York for 18 years and that principle of consistent visiting is one that he drills into his staff. So much around the children is changeable and inconsistent while this ministry is there for them faithfully 'whatever it takes.'

Fourthly, we saw *strong positive leadership*—leaders who spent time with staff and children getting to know their problems and time with God to solve their problems; leaders who did not ask anything of the staff that they were not prepared to do themselves; leaders who kept the vision. It helps having such a focussed objective with children but we all know how such objectives can easily multiply. The Americans go in for recognition and rewards. This happens at Metro Ministries among the staff. One evening we witnessed an extraordinary meeting where staff members were given small financial rewards for the number of children signed up for a particular programme. This was accompanied for the most part by affirming, encouraging personal tributes plus a mixture of silly prizes. All this was done in a humorous and positive manner. It raised a few questions in our minds but certainly the staff there loved it.

The emphasis is on positive reinforcement and it seems to work. At a weekly staff meeting that we sat in on, the assistant pastor shared a paper on 'Areas of concern for a leader.' He asked, 'How do we keep the best people with us?'

The answer included, 'Become better yourself; raise the standard of excellence and commitment; add value to the lives of quality people; offer significance and ownership.' The pastor challenged them to make time with people to know their problems and to spend time with God to solve those problems. And among this strong leadership there was no hiding of weaknesses, something that only served to connect people more closely within the team.

It also helps that Wilson and his staff live and sleep in the neighbourhood. 'This is our home. These people are our neighbours.'[3] They project an image of caring. They do provide food and clothing for needy families but they never seem to lose the focus on individual children. Wilson particularly recalls Jose who showed the leader his name carved into his stomach by his mother's latest lover. 'On that dismal stairway I realized that I did not come to New York's ghettos to reach ten thousand or even a hundred thousand children—I came for Jose. You see the masses. And you have to think in those terms. But the masses are made up of individuals.'[4]

3

A Typical Saturday Kidz Klub

The programme itself is fairly simple and straightforward, and is very flexible. As we grow more confident and familiar with the material we are increasingly changing and developing it to suit our children, situation, and our own team's strengths and weaknesses. As each adult congregation is unique, so each Kidz Klub will inevitably have its own style. What we offer below is our current pattern, which will doubtless continue to evolve.

The programme each Saturday lasts one-and-a-half hours. At first this seemed too long a period to keep the children interested, but anything less has left us omitting certain items or rushing through the teaching time.

The children arrive up to an hour before we open the doors. Most of the children arrive ten to fifteen minutes before we start, so we encourage leaders to spend time with the children. As they arrive they are lined up according to gender, and already at this stage we take responsibility for the children and begin to impose our standards of discipline. The programme is specifically aimed at 5- to 11-year-olds. Metro Ministries and Frontline have extended the age range to include 3-year-olds. They have split their programmes between 3- to 6-year-olds and 7- to 11-year-olds. At Page Moss we have so far stayed

3   B Wilson, *Whose Child is This?* (Charisma Life) p 72.
4   *Ibid* p 94.

with 5- to 11-year-olds.

As the children enter, in an orderly fashion, each child is registered. We consider this to be important as it allows visitors to have full, up to date information regarding the attendance records of the children they visit. In addition, first-time visitors give their name, address, telephone number and date of birth. Within the first two weeks of attendance, parents of new children will be asked to complete a 'Parental Consent Form,' which allows the visitor to introduce themselves, and hopefully assures the parents of our care and concern for the well being of their child.

After registration the children are escorted to their seats, ensuring that the smaller ones sit at the front, and that where appropriate certain children can be kept apart. As they come in two leaders will normally engage in dialogue from the stage, with a background of music. Then the lights are dimmed, the countdown begins, and it is time for Kidz Klub! The programme currently runs as follows:

Welcome—leaders enter the stage accompanied by lights, music, balloons and cheers!

Rules—these are sung!

> 'Rule number one is stay in your seat,
> Rule number two is obey your team captain, and
> Rule number three is the whistle means silence.'

It is essential that the rules are understood and strictly adhered to. Tough discipline is essential to control such large numbers of children, to avoid the few spoiling it for the many, and to enable vulnerable, hesitant children to view Kidz Klub as a place of safety and security. Unlike school, where for some of our children exclusion may be a preferable alternative, they do not want to miss Kidz Klub. In any case, we would rather work positively with one hundred responsive children, than lower the standards for a small minority that choose not to behave. Our expectations regarding behaviour are spelled out very clearly each week, and any disciplinary measures which need to be taken are explained to the child involved, and their parents. As yet, despite our firm policy, no child has been permanently excluded from Kidz Klub. It is often the biggest surprise to visitors how well the children listen and accept the discipline.

Opening prayer—a leader guides a child in prayer. This is seen as an honour, and places God at the centre of all that happens at Kidz Klub.

Praise—usually four or five fast, loud, action songs. All the children are expected to join in.

Games—the children are in two teams, boys against girls, and representatives take part in games. The issues of pitting boys against girls, and the use of competition, always raise questions. Although probably not politically correct, we are happy to stick with our current practice. Our line is that there is a need to teach children to be competitive without being aggressive and vindictive. We always encourage the losers of a good competition to cheer the winners. We certainly raise the competitive stakes but try hard not to go over the top. We have tried other ways of dividing the children into teams, but using gender works best. It makes administration less complicated, and helps foster the sense of belonging which is so important. Whenever a game is won, a burst of the victorious team's theme song is played, with the leaders and all the children doing the accompanying actions—currently 'We are family' for the girls and 'The boys are back in town' for the boys. At the end of the day it works for us. In America the younger age group are in mixed teams and the older ones are in boy/girl competition. The children are chosen because they can remember the previous week's memory verse, answer a question on the previous week's teaching, have coloured in their memory verse sheet particularly well, or can recite the 'four important things.' The games are often messy, energetic and exciting. The support is loud and enthusiastic.

The normal sequence is question, game one, question, game two, visit by guest character (Darth Vader and Scooby Doo have both appeared recently—this does not need to have any particular relevance, it is just good fun!), question, game three. The games time is not just great fun—it also reinforces the teaching of the previous week.

Four important things—will be brought into the programme each week. These are core values of Kidz Klub, and can be understood by all children:

1. God loves me
2. I have sinned
3. Jesus died for me
4. I must now decide to live for God.

In using repetition in this way there is always the danger of over-reliance on set formulae, of believing that as long as the children know these important truths they are okay, and even perhaps of opening ourselves to accusations of brain-washing. However, the use of set liturgy in church worship is not exactly innovative. There is a challenge in deciding how we come to a real understanding of these principles as both adults and children, which will prevent the Klub becoming dependent on fixed formulae and the leaders from becoming over-secure in an apparently successful club.

Talent spot—any child can come onto the stage and perform gymnastics, play a musical instrument, dance, yo-yo, act, mime, and sing. This highly supportive performing encourages and affirms each child.

Birthdays—celebrated noisily!

Basketball—children who bring friends have their names entered into a 'hat.' Those picked at random have the opportunity of scoring a basket, and winning a good quality prize. Maybe with a little more encouragement adults too might be persuaded to bring friends to church!

Game—after which the winning team celebrates, while the losers sportingly clap—sometimes!

Worship—one or two quieter, slower songs, which encourage the children to think more deeply about what Kidz Klub is really about. This section of the programme also helps the children to 'gear down' and settle before the teaching time.

Giving—to some appropriate, topical need. It is important that children understand that Christianity is not just about receiving, but also giving. Appropriate needs might be a current disaster (eg hurricane damage in Honduras), or an Eastern European orphanage. OHP or video pictures are important visual aids.

Review of the rules—during the teaching time extremely high standards of behaviour are demanded. Any children misbehaving, talking, distracting another child, or obviously not listening will be taken aside and warned. If this happens again, they will have a cross drawn on their hand and will not receive a sweet at the end of Kidz Klub. Collectively, the boys and the girls each have four balloons—each instance of bad behaviour results in one balloon being popped. If all of the boys' balloons are popped, the boys do not receive any sweets and, even worse, they are given instead to the girls!

Teaching time—this is made up of:

- **Lesson introduction**—which refers back to the previous week's teaching, and emphasizes the theme for the half term. This is important in preparing the children for the teaching to come.
- **Memory verse**—short, strong verses tend to work best. The sheets the visitors take to the children each week reinforce the memory verse.
- **Bible lesson**
- **3 or 4 object lessons**—these are creatively communicated using puppets, drama, characters, OHP, video, or slides.
- **Life story**—this continues from week to week, and helps the children to apply the lesson to real life situations.

Every week the teaching time contains a one-concept lesson, taken from the Bible, which is presented in a number of different ways. To hold the attention of children ranging from five years old to those in the early teenage years is not easy—but it is possible.

Orderly dismissal—those children who want a leader to pray privately with them wait as the other children leave. Leaders who are not needed to pray are encouraged to mingle outside the building for a short while.

The programme is varied but accessible to many children. Some, inevitably, will not like the noise, or the games, or the whole style of the programme, but

9

the children in our estate, who otherwise would never come near a church except to vandalize it, continue to attend faithfully and enthusiastically. This loud, magazine-style programme is an attempt to respond to the culture of today without compromising God's values and the message of salvation. Many of these children live in a disposable world where relationships are thrown out with their ready-made meals. It is therefore vital to show that the gospel, which is reliable, consistent and eternal, offers security in a fragile and broken world. We consistently attract children who have been excluded from mainline education. We readily accommodate children with special needs. We firmly believe that if we are going to see a transformation in this generation of children, then we have got to instil biblical values while they are still young. As Bill Wilson likes to say, 'It is a lot easier to make boys and girls than to repair men and women.' So our Kidz Klub programme is unashamedly, enthusiastically and deliberately Christian in its approach, content and presentation.

4

New York to Liverpool, Glasgow, Sheffield...

Metro Ministries are more than willing for their model of working with children to be given away. They do not want to exercise any quality control about what happens elsewhere or have any say in the way things are run. They would love to see a network of Kidz Klubs in every city around the world. They are in fact spreading across the States and abroad. Bill Wilson reckons from his travels that Frontline Kidz Klub in Liverpool would be in the top five from around the world. The core leaders at Frontline have visited New York on at least three occasions and some of them have been through an extended training programme at Metro Ministries. Frontline developed its Kidz Klub in this way—it is the result of six years of hard work, trial and error, as they have watched God 'build his church.'

Summer 1992	a holiday Bible Club is held at their former church building.
Sept 1992	a small weekly club is continued on a Tuesday night.
Spring 1994	after two more summer holiday clubs the weekly club is moved to a Saturday and they adopt Bill Wilson's model of weekly home visits for every child.
Sept 1995	Kidz Klub begins to use Bill Wilson's resource packs.
Feb 1996	Kidz Klub moves into a bigger building and the club continues to grow.
Easter 1997	Kidz Klub splits into a morning and an afternoon session

	to allow for growth.
Easter 1998	Kidz Klub splits into 'Tiny Tots' and 'Big Kids' to accommodate continued growth.
Sept 1998	The 'Edge' begins, a club for 11–16 year olds.

From 40 children a week they now regularly have as many as 700. They say that the real key has certainly been the weekly visits, which every child receives. A recent fact sheet revealed:

- *It costs £50 to hire a bus for each session of Kidz Klub. We currently use 6 double decker buses each week.*
- *There are 3 paid staff members each receiving £25 a week. There are over 40 volunteers working every Saturday.*
- *Nearly 1500 children get visited every single week.*
- *Whatever way you look at it something good is going on. But for this work to continue we need people to commit to give on a regular basis. We cannot keep up with the number of kids that want to come to church...It works out at about 75p a week for each child.*

First Impressions

When we first visited Frontline we were sceptical about the figures; we even counted to check up. Quickly it became apparent that the team made going to church an event. The children could not wait to be there because they did not know what was going to happen and they did not want to miss a thing. The building on the outside was an old army barracks but inside it seemed a cross between a 'Blue Peter' studio' and a Broadway set. Recently it was set up as a yellow submarine with water coming from unusual places. Basically Frontline have adopted the Bill Wilson model without much deviation. The use of buses is quite a new venture in the English scene. These buses go to areas such as Toxteth and Edge Hill. It is a massive investment in children, which is bearing fruit. Although it is now very professional they started with one worker who had a tub of sweets and a weekly budget of £5.

Visitors at Frontline receive a helpful two-page bulletin, which includes a section 'How we can help you.' They now supply Bill Wilson's resources in the UK and they are willing to help as much as they can. We found a visit from one of their leaders and repeated visits to Frontline very helpful in setting up our own Kidz Klub.

Beginnings

We started a pilot scheme with children from two after-school clubs that had lost direction. We made two scoreboards, used some black curtain to make the parish church less 'churchy,' and used the existing sound system. I mention these things because when people see the present set-up with staging, live band, lights and sound system they think it is too far from where they are starting from. We moved from the parish church to our Anglican/Methodist sister church in the most socially deprived part of the parish. Our connections with the four primary schools in the parish and the number of children on our doorstep mean that we have not felt it necessary to use buses. The building is already full on a Saturday morning and we have put in an offer for the buildings next door, at present a printer's shop. In our piloting period we used our own material but since our first move we have used the Bill Wilson material. The core team of seven has grown in confidence about adapting some of the material. Having seen some of the problems in New York such as drugs and violence, I think we are probably less dramatic now about the sin in our midst.

Moving Forwards

We have been offered a vehicle to develop the 'Sidewalk Sunday School' approach. We are considering the options but certainly the weather is against outdoor events for most of the year. We probably do not have the same sidewalk/pavement culture that they have in the USA nor do we have quite the high-density housing. We do know of outdoor schemes that run in Glasgow and in Hackney in the summer.

We anticipated that this 'Saturday church' would be entirely separate from what happens on a Sunday. We never anticipated that children would come back the next day, or if they did, we expected that as soon as they experienced something so different from Kidz Klub then they would not return. But more children than we imagined keep coming to church on Sunday as well. We are not entirely sure why. We suspect it is the love and individual attention that they are receiving from their Kidz Klub leaders. Although this way of working may still seem daunting for individual churches it may well be the way forward for a deanery or circuit.

Sheffield

St Thomas' Crookes has adopted a slightly different model in Sheffield. They run a midweek club along New York lines but this is only one aspect of a bigger strategy, which also encompasses a lively and dynamic Kidz Church for Sunday mornings, termly events and a schools' outreach. They are working towards a structure that will draw kids from the schools via the termly events into the midweek club and then will take them on either into Kidz Church or into their teenage programme. They believe that smaller midweek clubs running from local churches will be more effective than running one central venue to which kids are bused. In Glasgow YWAM have been setting up various Kidz Klubs. Their next phase has been to run Children's *Alpha* groups in the homes of Christian families.

Prizes

Perhaps one of the American influences that we have struggled with is the whole area of prize giving. The Americans spend an enormous amount of money on prizes. They also give cash prizes to children and financial incentives to their staff. Frontline has again followed the Americans with top prizes of football kits, a great incentive to soccer-mad Liverpudlians. To many, the prize-giving has a ring of bribery about it. It helps persuade the children to come and participate. Our own observation is that without the very best of holiday club activity, the most up-to-date methods of communication and the positive, loving relationships nurtured by weekly visiting, then the prizes would not be sufficient in themselves. We do not give away any cash prizes. If a child brings a friend and is fortunate to be drawn out of the hat to have a free throw at the basketball, then they stand a chance of winning a 'Walkman,' a new basketball or toys. The first girl to win a Walkman came from a household where the adults are into drugs. She would not come anywhere near a traditional Sunday school, but she did travel over a mile to come to Kidz Klub.

Where Next?

The question arises, 'What next after Kidz Klub?' We have discovered that neither Metro Ministries nor Frontline are very strict with the cut off at age eleven. Providing they were in the club to start with and are not misbehaving the children are allowed to stay on. The programmes we have seen in New York and Frontline for the early teens seem to use quite a lot of video. We have also been impressed with the 'Rock Solid' programme developed by British Youth for Christ. Experimentation with this material in our local comprehensive school has proved positive, reaching 50–70 young people every week. Our Schools worker had to go down to Northampton to be trained in the use of the programme and he seems confident that this could well provide the basis for the next step after Kidz Klub. The 'Rock Centre' in Belfast has a good record of linking their club work with roadshows in schools. Their Christmas '98 event at a leisure centre attracted 1200 children. It involved them in hiring 26 buses.

We would be foolish to say that the Kidz Klub recipe of a fast-moving mix of worship, drama, competitions and one-issue talks appeals to every child. Our experience is that it attracts a wide cross-section. Interestingly in Liverpool it seems to appeal best to what we call the 'scallies' (short for scallywags). The primary school nearest to Trinity Church, where our Kidz Klub is held, has over 70% of the children eligible for free school meals. In other words we are reaching kids that previously we were a long way from making any impact on at all. The Lambeth Conference stated that teams of adults and young people in as many congregations as possible be trained for holistic ministry to young people outside the church, so as to speak of God's love in Christ in ways that can be heard. The bishops also stressed recognition of the faithful and creative work by many church members with children both within and beyond the church's borders. We hope, therefore, that they may examine the Bill Wilson model in the light of their affirmation and commitment to children and young people.

5

The Power of Personal Visiting—
The Heart of Kidz Klub

All visitors to Metro Sunday School New York are plainly told, 'The visitation is the most important aspect of the ministry here. It takes precedence over everything else. Regardless of what other work needs to be done, visiting our children is more important. It is our reason for being here.'[5]

Relationships do not just happen. In some churches they never happen. Relationships need to be developed, cultivated, worked at and nurtured. With our children, relationships grow through a powerful and consistent presence in the kids' lives over a long period of time. This is primarily accomplished through personal visiting, which in reality is the foundation of the whole ministry.

Three questions need to be addressed—why, how and who?

1. Why Do We Visit?

It is no secret that most church members are white, middle class and comfortable. If you are not when you enter, then the influence of the church will soon touch you in this way! The question of how we are to enter the vastly different world of the masses around is a key issue as we enter the new millennium. How can I, with my secure family background, good education, comfortable financial situation and supportive friends, even begin to empathize with a girl of seven, who through no fault of her own shares her home with adults who are addicted to drugs, who sees theft not as crime but as survival, school as a luxury which takes a backseat compared to the more pressing needs of caring for three younger siblings, and for whom Jesus Christ is as real as Father Christmas, the Tooth Fairy or Mickey Mouse? I cannot live in her world, but I can walk through it with her. It is impossible to visit children, to see their homes, 'families' and lifestyles, and not be moved to tears. Our children need people who are willing to be vulnerable enough to come and place themselves in someone else's world at the risk of being hurt—mentally, physically or emotionally. When that is done on a consistent basis, something happens to both the giver and the receiver.

For many children, our visit is the highlight of the week. At first, many are bemused—if we have not come to collect money, or to complain about their behaviour, why are we there? The idea that an adult is making the effort to visit them simply because they are worth visiting is astounding. It comes as a surprise to many children that an adult can chat to them without shouting,

5   Email from Guest Relations dept. Metro Ministries.

swearing or being abusive. The regular person-to-person contact is a unique affirming event in their lives.

Visiting is not easy. The area around our Kidz Klub has been a no-go area for many church members. Our visitors are not used to observing drug deals, witnessing community justice being administered, or walking around an area where police normally venture only in protected vehicles manned by 'snatch squads.' But visiting helps to break down the barriers *within us*. If we become alienated from the very people we seek to reach, we cannot minister effectively.

Everyone in our community knows about Kidz Klub. Our visitors are recognized, respected and welcomed. Our buildings, vehicles and staff suffer less from vandalism. People do not care how much you know, until they know how much you care. Personal visiting has proven to be an extremely effective way of bringing the love of Christ into our desperate community. In three months we have seen an increase in families bringing children for baptism and thanksgiving, have shared in the pain of bereavement, depression, and unemployment, have been able to greet new arrivals into our community, have offered hope, comfort, love and vision to a despairing, hurt, empty and abandoned community.

2. How Do We Visit?

Our 'reason' for visiting is to hand out a sheet, with the week's memory verse printed on it. Children are encouraged to colour them in, with the best ones being awarded prizes. For most of us, 'cold' visiting would be difficult and ineffective, but we can all hand over a sheet of paper! We tend to visit in pairs, for security, to cover for illness, to provide prayer support, and because Jesus recommended it. The key is that visiting is not something we fit in to our busy timetable when we have a spare hour. It is an absolute priority. The time is fixed in our diaries, and is only changed when it is absolutely necessary. Children, and parents, *know* when we are going to visit, regardless of the weather or the temperature—and this serves to emphasize the importance that we give to our children. It is impossible to exaggerate the immense impact upon a child who feels unloved, insignificant and worthless, when they see that someone has ventured out in the pouring rain, to visit *them*. What a wonderful expression of the compelling love of Jesus.

3. Who Visits?

People who have an active leadership role in the Kidz Klub programme have to take part in the visiting. In order to ensure that Kidz Klub consistently relates to the children, its leaders have to enter into the children's lives through visiting. The right to lead, teach or pray with the children has to be earned. Respect is not given lightly. Trust grows slowly. Children have been deeply hurt by adults, and the onus is on leaders to demonstrate their faithful love for the children through visiting. For us, initially, visiting was the hardest part of the week, but it has now become one of the highlights. The joyful excitement of the children as they run to greet us, the warmth of the parents, the frequent opportunities to listen, to understand and to share something of Jesus' love with people whom we would otherwise probably never have met, combines to make visiting a privilege and a pleasure.

To quote Bill Wilson again, 'We all want a personal visitation from the Lord. So often it comes through personal visitation *for* the Lord.'[6]

6
You Can Do It!

'Where can you find people willing and able to *do* this? Where did you find the helpers you needed? How did you get them enthused? Involved? Trained?' This was one valid response to our enthusiastic description of the Kidz Klub model. Many church members suffer from tiredness, frustration and pressure. Others gave up trying years ago. Yet others are afraid to offer their services for fear of condemning themselves to a life sentence of hard labour! So how can any church, or group of churches, realistically launch into yet another new time-, energy- and resource-hungry area of ministry?

1. Acknowledge the Need

If your church has a thriving children's ministry, which is successfully impacting the local community, and producing young disciples of Jesus, then why would you even consider changing things? On the other hand, if you belong to the vast majority of churches, who look back with longing to the golden days of packed Sunday Schools, and lament the marginal influence you are currently able to exert on the local community, and if you can readily identify the need to explore a new way of reaching the vast numbers of children in your area who have little or no meaningful contact with Jesus or his representatives, then read on.

Can you identify with the sentiments of a previous Grove booklet, which stated 'we are dealing with a whole generation without eternal hope, a generation that has not heard the Christian story about a heavenly Father who loves them. Disaster awaits...'[7] Do you long to take God to your children and bring your children to God? Can you see that something has to change? George

---

6 B Wilson quoted in *Ministries Today*, Sept 1991.
7 Penny Frank and Geoff Pearson, *Too Little Too Late* (Grove Evangelism Series No 41, Cambridge: Grove Books, 1998) p 3.

Barna, in a chapter entitled 'A vision for spiritual renewal' describes how a church responds to the need for change. 'We reprioritize our activities, set different goals, develop new relationships, and reallocate our resources so that we may take advantage of emerging opportunities and alternatives.'[8] Genuinely acknowledging the need for change is the essential first step in this process. Do not start a Kidz Klub because it is fashionable, or because the church down the road runs one. Do not adopt the model half heartedly, 'to see if it works.'

When a group of us attended a Bill Wilson conference in February 1998, we were keen to soak up the 'how-to lessons' of Kidz Klub and to gain a practical understanding of the way it works. Our frustration increased with every session as he plugged away at emphasizing that first we need to share a burden. He talked of God's compassion for the lost children, and of our need to have the heart of a shepherd. Once we have reached that stage, he reasoned we would surely do something, and why not try the Kidz Klub model?

Assuming you see the need to enter a new phase in your ministry to and with children, how do you proceed?

2. Identify a Core Team

We have a Core Team of seven, who meet each week to plan the programme for the coming Saturday and to look at other, wider, Kidz Klub-related issues. We pray, plan and share together. The Core Team members are the vision carriers, the ones who have the drive, the compassion, the ability and the energy to make Kidz Klub happen. The primary qualification for being a Core Team member is God's calling to this particular ministry. Most of us have had to let go of other ministries. Core Team members must have a God-given compassion for the children, which enables them to visit on dark, wet winter evenings, and to consistently maintain the high levels of commitment necessary to run a Kidz Klub. These people will be at the same time excited, challenged, and probably frightened by the Kidz Klub model. They will be aware of its powerful potential, and of the exacting level of commitment it demands.

The Core Team does not need to be large. In New York the Sidewalk Sunday Schools each attract over 100 children (plus a number of parents) yet are run by just three staff members. Kidz Klub is largely an up-front presentation, and the relationship-building takes place during the visiting. Consequently, fewer leaders are needed than at an after-school club, for example, where relationships are developed primarily through participating in activities with small groups of children.

Core Team members have both shared and individual responsibilities. As well as sharing overall leadership, each member visits children every week. Individual areas of responsibility cover items such as the weekly programme, visiting, music (both live and recorded), general administration, and so on.

---

8   G Barna. *The Second Coming of the Church* (Word) p 129.

Other tasks are allocated according to ability and availability. We also have a 'Team Leader' who does not attend Core Team meetings and is not usually concerned with the detailed planning, though he does have a visiting round. He is responsible for the overall vision and direction of the ministry, and works closely with the Core Team, providing much needed spiritual leadership and experience.

It will be necessary to identify Core Team members. Some will be people who have proven in the past to have the required compassion, ability and stamina to engage in children's ministry. Others will be motivated by the Kidz Klub model and will become involved in working with children for the first time. As well as having some gifting, the most important requirement is the sense of God's calling to this particular ministry. Core Team members must regard Kidz Klub as their number one priority.

3. Share the Vision

The excitement and enthusiasm of the Core Team will be infectious. There will be other people who will be keen to engage in this exciting ministry, with its vast potential for growth. We took people already working with children to see another Kidz Klub. Together with them we looked realistically at what we were doing, and we shared with them our desire to improve our ministry with children. We gained their permission to change, and, perhaps, to fail. We tried hard to channel both new and existing leaders into new areas of ministry. We ran a three day Kidz Klub-style Holiday Club, which 'captured' a good number of young leaders, as they became enthusiastic about what they were experiencing. We received prophetic words offering further encouragement, and on one occasion the congregation literally wept together over the children, and our frustration at the little progress we had made.

Not everyone was convinced, but a few months after starting our Kidz Klub we have few detractors. Our Kidz Klub invariably attracts a 'congregation' more than twice the size of our Sunday congregation. Those who were sceptical at first, who prophesied 'it won't work here,' quickly and graciously changed their views. Established members of the church rapidly came to see Kidz Klub as the future of the local church in our area. For the first time in over a generation the church building is regularly filled to capacity with children, worshipping God and receiving life-giving teaching. Kidz Klub may not be successful in every location all the time, but our experience has been that it works, so there will be no need to whip up enthusiasm. 'A great leader does not manipulate people through personal charisma, entrancing speeches, or empty promises. Great leaders motivate people through the delivery of honest substance.'[9] Many of our current helpers initially came along 'just to watch' but found themselves moved and excited and ended up joining the team of helpers.

9   G Barna, *The Second Coming of the Church* p 165.

4. Bear the Cost

Running a Kidz Klub demands time, energy, people and resources. These do not instantly materialize! It may well be necessary for a church to make a thorough evaluation of its current children's work. It is inevitable that some activities will have to stop altogether, especially if most of your 'best' workers are already fully occupied. We shut down two after-school clubs, and staff members and others created time in their already busy schedules. For most churches, Kidz Klub will not be an addition to the existing children's work; rather it will become the main focus of ministry with children. This may seem 'a bridge too far,' but often those faithful workers, whom we rightly want to avoid offending or hurting, will be relieved that their burden is to be removed. They will hopefully be delighted to see the increased importance given to children, and will be able to see their work as the platform on which Kidz Klub can build.

It may be that painful decisions need to be made. We have seen the number of children we are reaching multiply tenfold in a few months, and there is vast potential for more growth. The risk is worth taking. We believe that people will find the time, energy and resources to plough into something worthwhile. Church members have in many instances been battered, by perceived (or actual) failure, into adopting a 'siege mentality.' This condition is life threatening but not inoperable! 'If we blend people's spiritual frustration with a clearly articulated and appealing spiritual alternative, there is incredible potential to ignite widespread, positive life transformation.'[10] It is amazing how we all manage to find the time to do the things we really want to do! (The authors usually manage to find time if tickets for a football match involving Liverpool or Hull City become available!) Kidz Klub is the most personally rewarding ministry many of us have been involved in, and has established itself as the highlight of the week.

As leaders of the two main churches involved at Trinity and Roby we have been criticized for having an obsession with children. It is a criticism that one of the authors and Penny Frank received following the publication of their Grove booklet highlighting the crisis in children's evangelism. At one time we would have defended ourselves against the negative implications of the word 'obsession.' Now we are happy to have that label. Why? Because it reveals our passion for souls and a deep caring for children. It is our ministry and we want to speak of it with a fervent passion. Yes, lots of other things still happen and other ministries have developed but this Kidz Klub ministry is something that has the commitment of our hearts. If you do not share our obsession then we hope that as Christians you are passionate about some other area of ministry in which you believe.

---

10 G Barna, *The Second Coming of the Church* p 198.

7
Great Fun—But Is It Church?

What is the purpose of the church? Most would agree that the Bible highlights four ingredients—worship, fellowship, nurture and evangelism. John Stott, in an exegesis of Acts 2.42–47 lists the four primary characteristics of a vital church:

- Worship that expresses the reality of the living God and joyfully celebrates Christ's victory over sin and death.
- Preaching and teaching that faithfully expounds the Word of God while relating to the burning issues of the day and to the pressing needs of the people.
- Caring and supportive relationships between individuals, Christ and one another.
- Outreach into the surrounding community that is imaginative, sensitive and compassionate.[11]

1. Worship

Worship involves giving to God the place of honour that is rightfully his, acknowledging him for who he is, and offering praise and petition. At its best, worship allows us to experience intimacy with our God. Expected ingredients in a normal church setting would incl1lude singing, liturgy, prayer, sacraments and an offering!

The Kidz Klub programme includes an energetic 'praise' time, with high-volume, fast-paced singing, and later, a time of gentler worship. The children praise Jesus with enthusiasm, engaging body, mind and spirit in worship. Clapping, lifting hands, praising, shouting and dancing are all biblical expressions of worship—their joy-filled expressiveness should not be mistaken for shallow emotionalism or meaningless activity.

The liturgy is unwritten—though the consistency of the programme gives the Kidz Klub a sense of direction and purpose. Singing the rules, recalling the *four important things*' or singing 'Happy Birthday' may never enter a new prayer book, but for the children they become an integral part of their church experience.

Prayer, both corporate and individual, constitutes a vital part of the programme. The session begins with a child leading in prayer, and ends with opportunities for those who wish to do so to share concerns with leaders, and take part in a time of personal prayer.

---

11 From taped lecture, quoted by L J Morris, *The High Impact Church* (Touch Publ) p 122.

The place of sacraments in Kidz Klub is yet to be fully explored. Both Metro Ministries and Frontline practice adult baptism only and therefore the question of baptizing children who attend Kidz Klub is not such an immediate issue. We are thinking along the lines of baptism and its meaning in terms of commitment. This pledge of commitment in the imagery of 1 Peter 3.21 may well be part of the step when a youngster moves on from Kidz Klub to become a helper or to join the next age group. Obviously if young people are ready to respond to the challenge then we will talk to them and their family. If they have already been baptized as a child then we will speak of repentance, faith and confirmation. We see Kidz Klub as an important part of the Christian journey and we will have to work out how baptism is to be the sacrament of that journey. It may well become clearer as through our visiting we make contact with families. Certainly Frontline has seen conversions from parents as a result of building on contacts from Kidz Klub.

Who should baptize in these circumstances? Michael Green writes, 'Liturgical functions such as baptism and presiding at the eucharist were not at that time restricted to any particular group of Christians. Perhaps they should not be today, so long as the administrant in either case is a respected and godly member of the congregation. There is no suggestion anywhere in the New Testament that baptism and the celebration of the Communion are tasks reserved for a priestly cadre.'[12] Obviously we must respect the disciplines of our faith community. I think, however, that church leaders will be wise to include the Kidz Klub leaders, either those most up-front, or the personal visitor of a child, in any preparation.

The children are encouraged to bring gifts of money, no matter how small, to help those in far worse situations. It is important that they learn that Christianity is about both receiving and giving.

2. Preaching and Teaching

Visitors to Kidz Klub are usually most impressed by the near-perfect silence, which accompanies the 20–30 minutes of Bible-based teaching. The lesson is normally one point, reinforced by being presented in numerous different ways. Use of drama, OHP, video projector, object lessons, slides, characters and story ensure that the strong message is received with interest. Our first ten weeks of Kidz Klub explored the Ten Commandments, containing clear, counter-cultural messages, faithful to the original yet applied to the everyday reality of the children's lives.

3. Care and Support

In the fragmented lives of most of our children, Kidz Klub has rapidly become one of the few stable, supportive, positive experiences. The sense of community, family, and belonging has deepened with a speed and strength

---

12 Michael Green, *To Corinth with Love* (Hodder) p 38.

we had not anticipated. To say that we, as leaders, love our children is not a boast; it is a fact.

The weekly visiting, discussed at length elsewhere, is key in this aspect of Kidz Klub. Through the consistent, faithful, prioritized visiting relationships develop with even the most withdrawn children, and the most suspicious or even hostile parents. Every individual child knows that somebody cares, and that somebody is willing to make the effort. They come to understand that in God's eyes they matter.

Outreach

Our growth, from 20 to 200 members in just three months, has been solely through children inviting their friends. We have used no other means of advertising, though we could have done so. The children are positively encouraged to bring friends—any that do so may have a turn at basketball and if successful win a prize. Clearly, though, it is the excellence of the programme, alongside the benefits of the visiting, which enables the children to bring their friends with confidence. Kidz Klub is unashamedly Christian from beginning to end, yet week after week the most unlikely children gladly bring their mates to join the fun. Inevitably the visiting means that the influence of Kidz Klub stretches into households, families and the wider community. There are clear opportunities to organize special evangelistic events for other family members, who can be fed into *Alpha* groups and so on. The relational basis of Kidz Klub both encourages and enables mission.

Kidz Klub does not look, feel or sound like church as we know it. But should we expect it to or demand that it does? After all, Jesus commanded us all to 'become like little children' (Matthew 18.3). Traditional church? Certainly not. But an authentic, biblical, relevant model of church? Absolutely. George Barna identifies three concerns that govern the decisions people make when choosing their place of worship—relevance, relationships, and practical benefits.[13] Using these criteria we commend Kidz Klub as an appropriate model of church for the children of today.

---

13 G Barna, *The Second Coming of the Church* p 130.

8
Appendix

Questions most commonly asked:

1. Where can we obtain resources for Kidz Klub?

Frontline Church will provide resources under the banner of Kidz Klub Trading. Telephone Celia Morris on 0151 733 7737 for a catalogue.

2. Are visitors welcomed at Metro Ministries New York, and do we have to go to New York to see how it works?

Yes, visitors are made welcome—contact Cheryl Najjar, Guest Relations Coordinator, email address MetroSSNY@aol.com, phone 718-453-3352. Please bear in mind that they are extremely focused on the children, so do not expect to receive too much attention. They prefer visitors to come Tuesday to Sunday. Their rules appear quite heavy and strict but are appropriate because of the area in which the Ministry is located. In addition it is possible to attend a Metro Ministries Brooklyn Boot Camp for one week which includes hands-on experience and training. There are also opportunities to work and train over longer periods as a volunteer.

For some the New York model will be too much, and in any case lack of time or finance will make it inaccessible. Frontline, Liverpool (contact Celia Morris 0151 733 7737) welcomes visitors as does Trinity Church, Page Moss, Liverpool (contact Philip Clark, 22 Easton Road, L36 4PB, 0151 489 6399, email philip@baruch.force9.co.uk).

3. What are the implications of the Children Act for Kidz Klub?

Unless your club meets for more than two hours it is unlikely that you will need to register with the Social services. However, contact with the Social Services Registration Department is advisable, as there are different interpretations of the Children Act in different regions. Do check your insurance especially concerning your adult visitors. Remember too health and safety issues including first aid and fire regulations. Most denominations now have particular individuals who act as Child Protection Advisors. Do consult them about policy and procedures. If you are into transporting children then do check seat belt regulations. Beware of just accepting transport that is suddenly offered to you. New regulations in 1999 are proving costly for some of the groups who bus children to their activities.

4. Is this children's evangelism or is it planting a children's church?

It is both. The children's church needs to be constantly outward looking and the evangelists must be aware of how children are going to be discipled. Both are interested in children being saved.

5. Do the present Sunday School teachers see it as a threat?

Certainly in the early days at Frontline this happened. When those leaders left, the present Sunday School leaders were well aware of the direction of the ministry and happy to complement the work among children. In our situation time was invested in winning the support of existing children's workers. Our Sunday School has been boosted considerably through Kidz Klub. The children we are reaching through Kidz Klub are not generally the type who would previously have gone near a church.

6. Where are Bill Wilson's adults now?

Some of them are in leadership positions. Many of them attend services on a Sunday. Wilson is honest about the effect on the children's lives. 'Only one out of every four young people are going to make it in life.' He adds, 'I'm also interested in what they do not become. I want to keep them out of the gutter; success to me is that they are not on Flushing Avenue with the hookers—or down on Troutman selling crack. That is why we work as hard at this as we do.'[14]

---

14 Quoted in *Alpha* Magazine, December 1993.